QUILT BLOCKS 1
GEOMETRIC PATTERNS I

KYOTO SHOIN

QUILT BLOCKS 1

1500 Illustrations in Color
GEOMETRIC PATTERNS I

はじめに

古い時代から洋の東西を問わず生活の必需品であった「キルト（布団の意）」。

やがて、豊かになり、人をおおうのに十分な大きさ、つまり、布織りの経済的な大きさ以上のサイズが求められるようになりました。

そこで、その時々に入手可能な布の幅や使用可能な布の分量を工夫し、不足する布を縫い合わせることで補いながら、さまざまな「キルト」のスタイルがうまれました。

特に掛け布団として使われる上掛け部分は、布を縫い合わせて大きさを補うだけでなく、装飾性も重要視されるようになりました。

例えば日本の伝統的な掛け布団の布のアレンジもこうして出来上がった様式といえましょう。

なかでも、いわゆる「アメリカン・パッチワーク・キルト」または「アメリカン・キルト」と呼ばれるキルトの装飾技法は、ヨーロッパの伝統的な手法をなぞりつつも、その表面デザインの過剰な展開と布使いの豊穣さに際だつことが特色で、この広がりは今に及んでいます。

本書では、アメリカン・キルトを中心に、布を縫い合わせて作られたデザイン・ブロックを取り出し、サンプリングしてみました。

普通、2m四方内外の大きさのキルトを見るとつい見落としがちな、構成要素としてのデザイン単位を改めて抜き出すことで、読む人の新たな発見や発想をうながすことを意図して企画しました。

近年アメリカの伝統工芸であるキルトに、より身近に接する機会を得た。

アメリカでのビジネス経験以来、アメリカの生活文化に少なからず親しみを持ち続けていたが、キルトの発見は新鮮だった。

建国後百年以上国の基幹産業のひとつであった木綿布を使い、アメリカの無名の女性達が美しい花を咲かせたのである。

現在、日本を始めアジア、ヨーロッパにも愛好者が多いという。

生活者の心を豊かにし、国を超えたネット・ワークを広げるキルトには、音楽、スポーツ、レジャーと共通する人を魅了する何かがあるのだろう。

河島 博

R ecentry I had the opportunity to become acquainted with the traditional American handicraft of Quilt.

Through my business experience in the U.S. I have learned much about American lifestyle and culture, but my discovery of Quilts was refreshing.

Based in the tradition of cotton fabric, a basic industry for over 100 years since the founding of the country, quiltmaking flowered at the hands of countless women across American.

Now I am told that quiltmaking is popular not only in Japan but across Asia and Europe.

I think that perhaps this is because there is something about Quilts that crosses borders, enriching one's life and touching people with a common interest in music, sports, and leisure.

河島 博 (かわしま・ひろし) ダイエー副会長

Hiroshi Kawashima Executive Vice Chairman The Daiei, Inc.

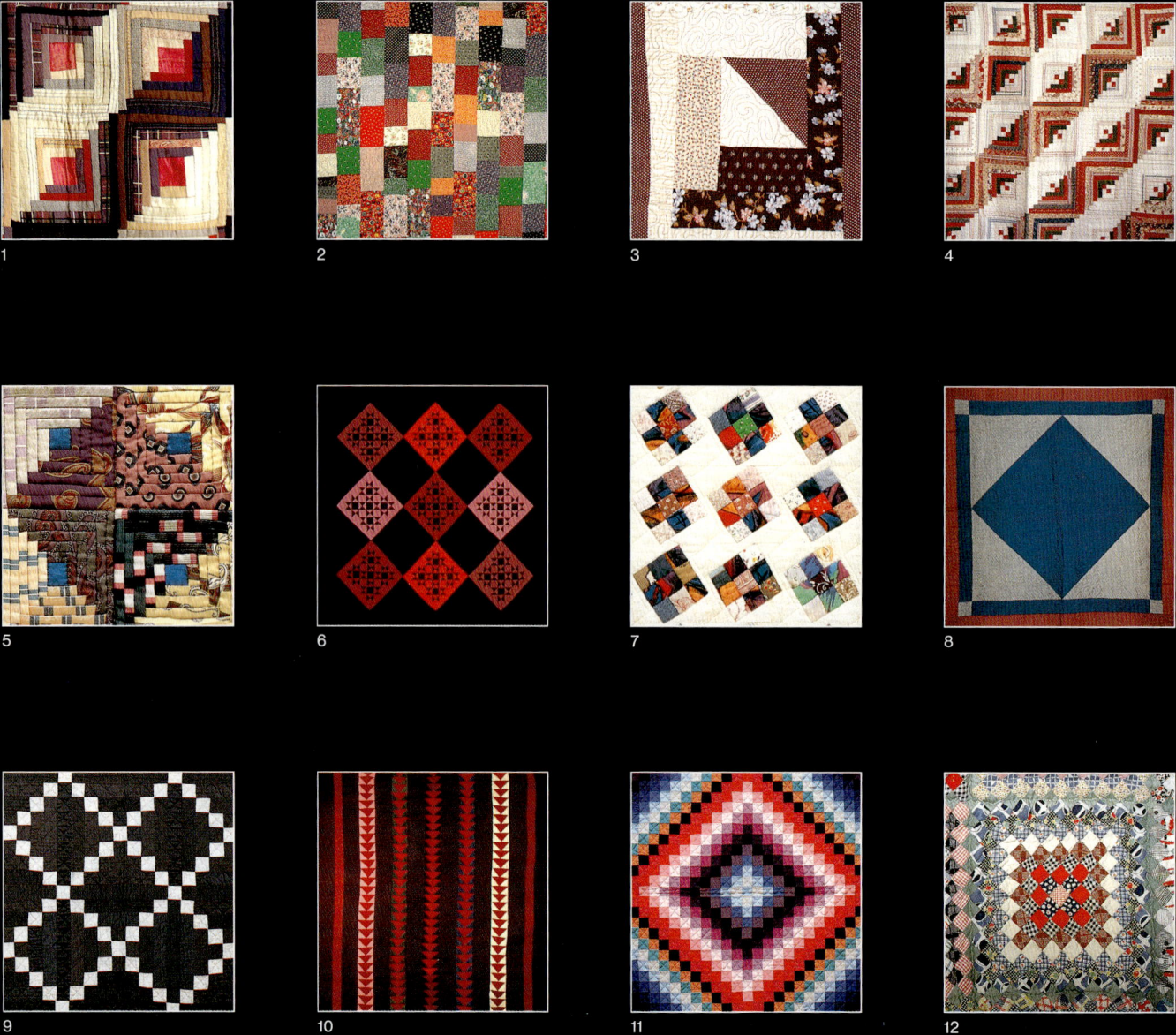

13

14

15

16

17

18

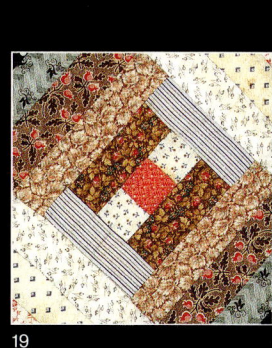
19

20

21

22

23

24

26

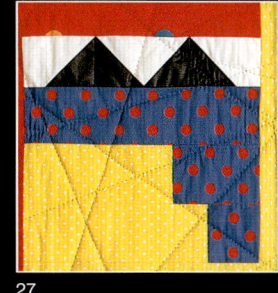
27

28

29

30

31

32

33

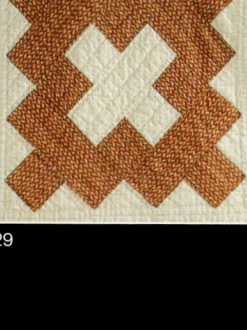
34

35

36

37

39

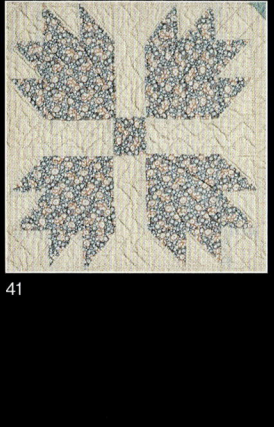

40

41

42

43

44

45

46

47

48

49

50

52

53

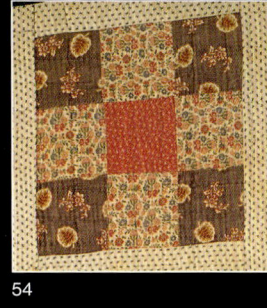
54

55

56

57

58

59

60

61

62

63

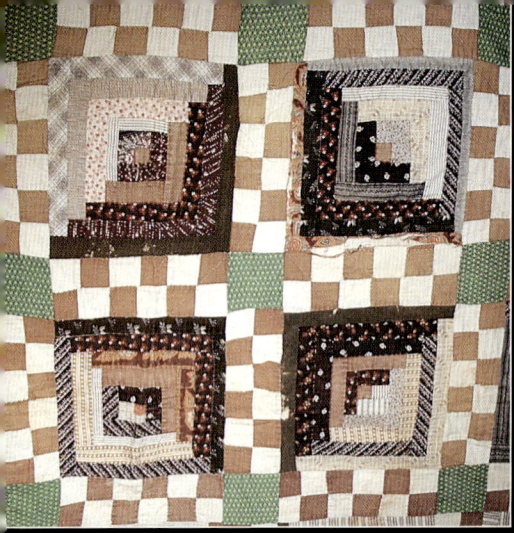

64

65

66

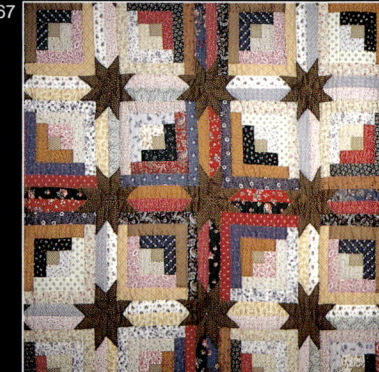

67

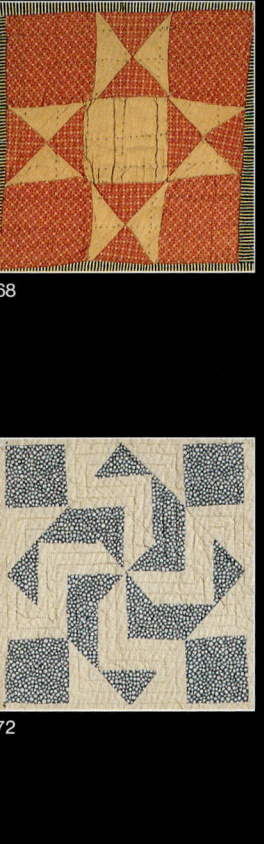
68

69

70

71

72

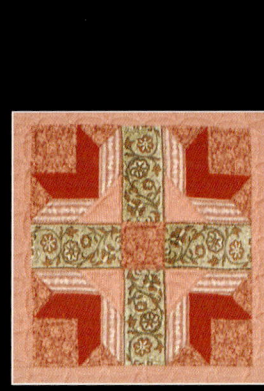
73

74

75

76

77

78

79

80

81

82

83

84 85 86 87

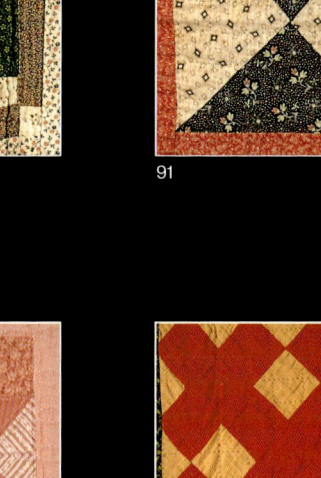

88 89 90 91

92 93 94 95

97

98

99

100

101

102

103

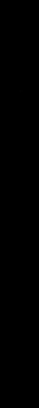

104

105

106

107

108

110

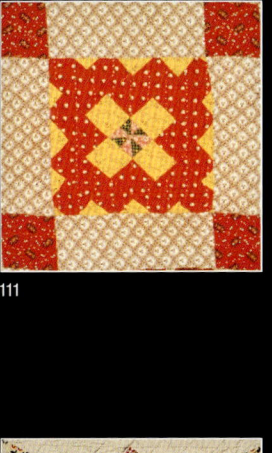
111

112

113

114 115 116

117

118

119

120 121

123 124 125 126

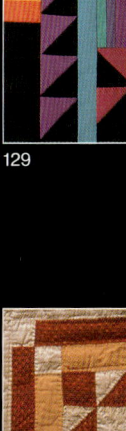

127 128  129 130

131 132 133 134

136

137

138

139

140

141

142

143

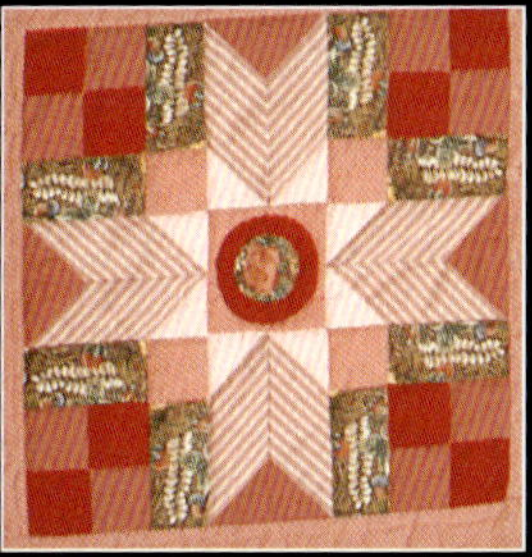

145

146

147

144

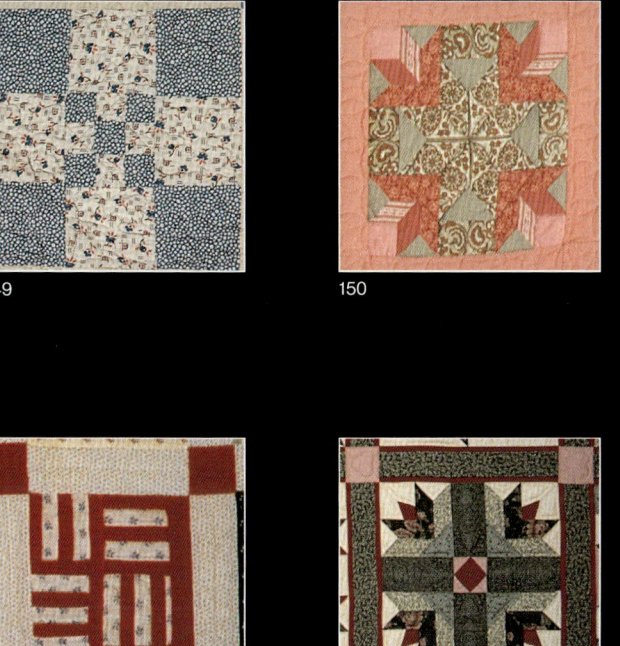

149

150

151

152

153

154

155

156

157

158

159

160

161

162

163

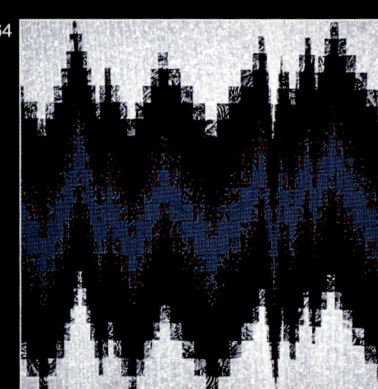

164

165

166

167

168

169

170

171

172

173

174

175

176

178

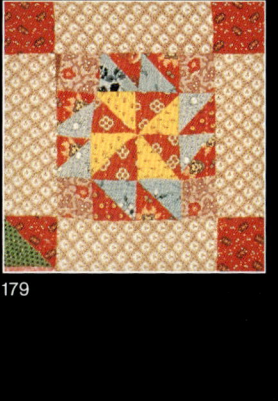
179

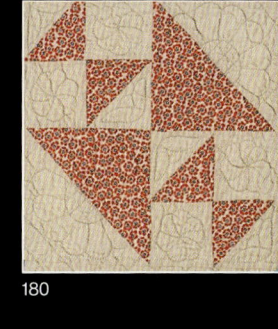
180

181

182

184

184

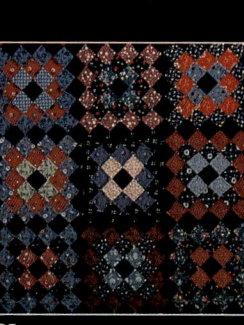
185

186

187

188

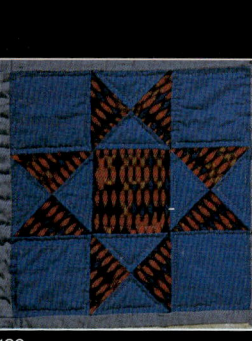
189

191

192

193

194

195

196

97

198

199

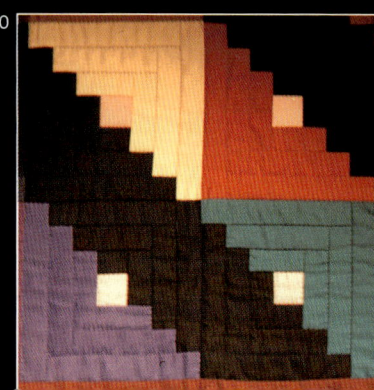

200

201

202

203

204

205

206

207

208

209

210

211

212

213

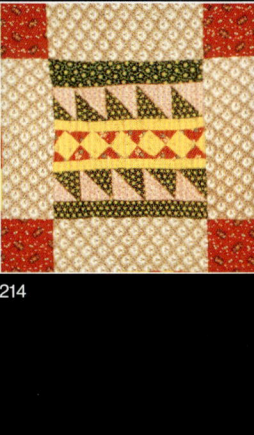

214

215

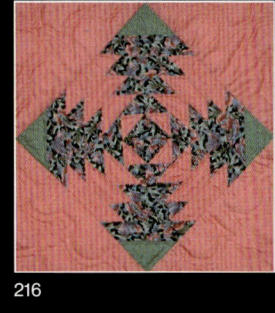

216

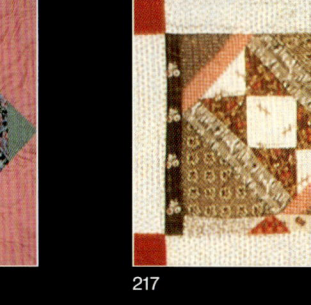

217

218

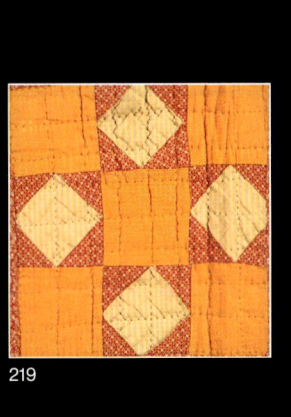

219

220

221

222

223

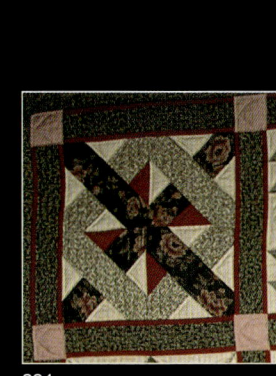

224

225

226

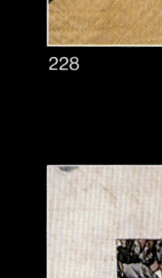

227

228

229

230

231

232

233

234

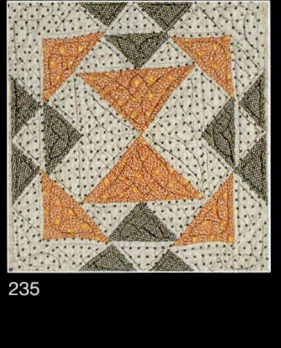

235

236

237

238

239

240

241

242

243

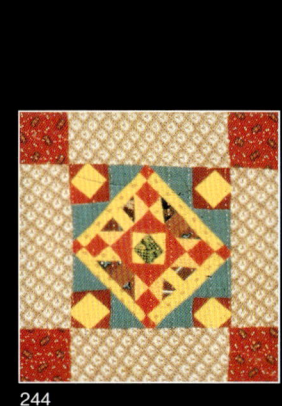

244

245

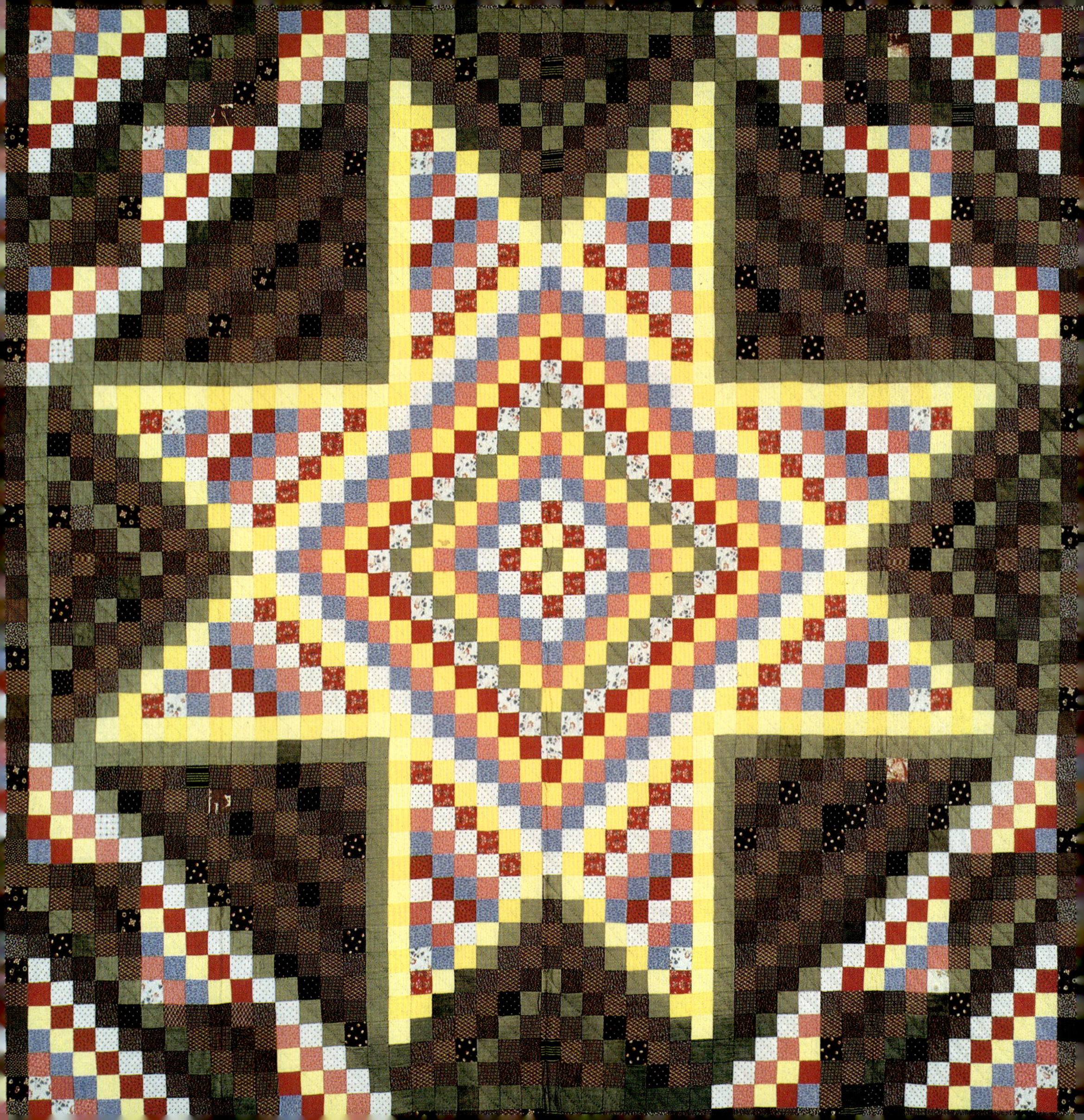

247 248 249 250

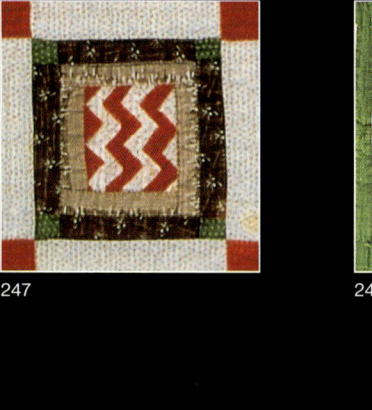

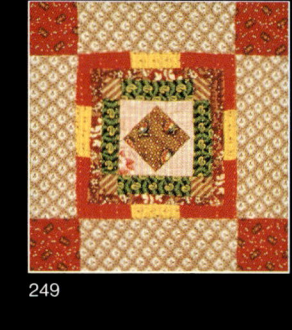

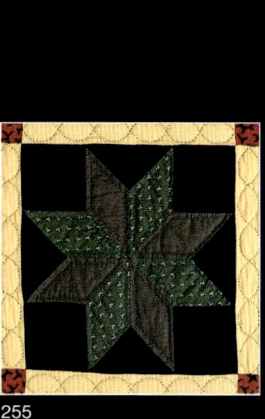

251 252 253 254

255 256 257 258

259

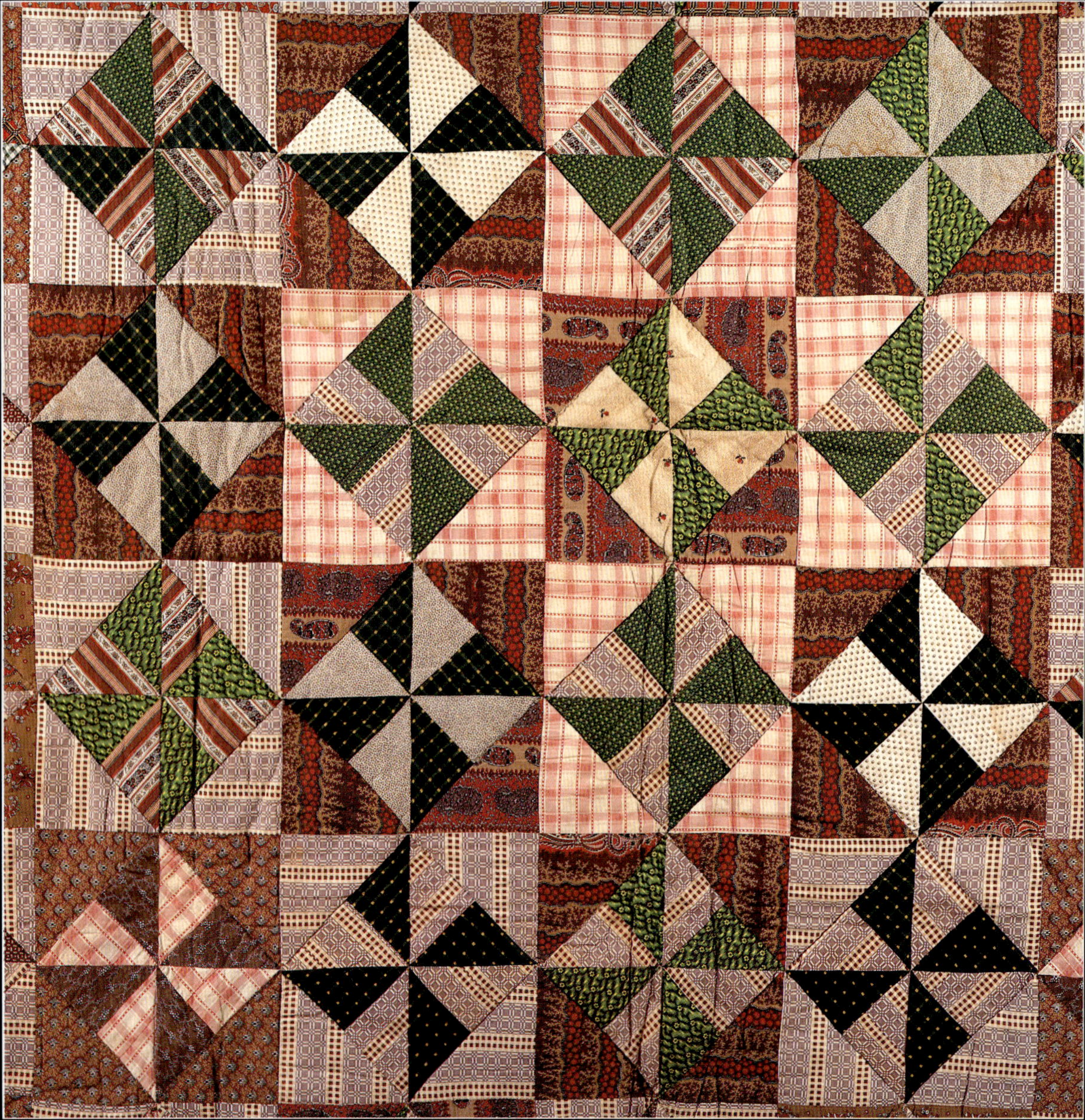

260
261
262
263
264
265
266
267
268
269
270
271

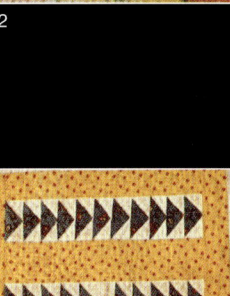

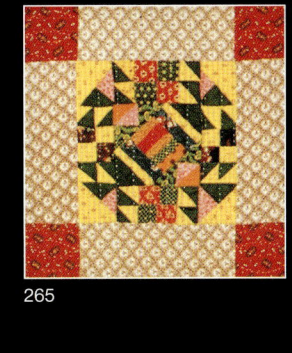

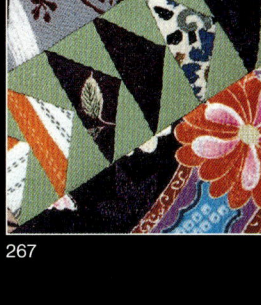

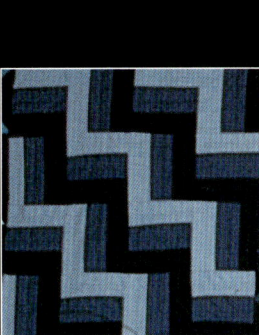

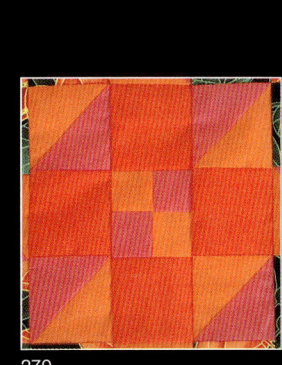

272

273

274

275

276

277

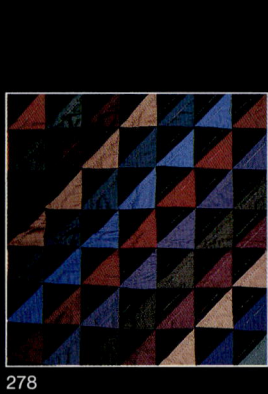

278

279

280

281

282

283

284

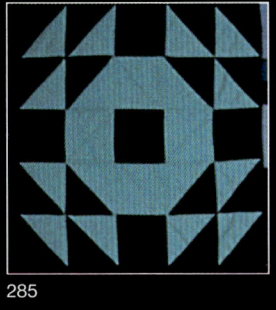

285

286

287

288

289

290

291

292

293

294

295

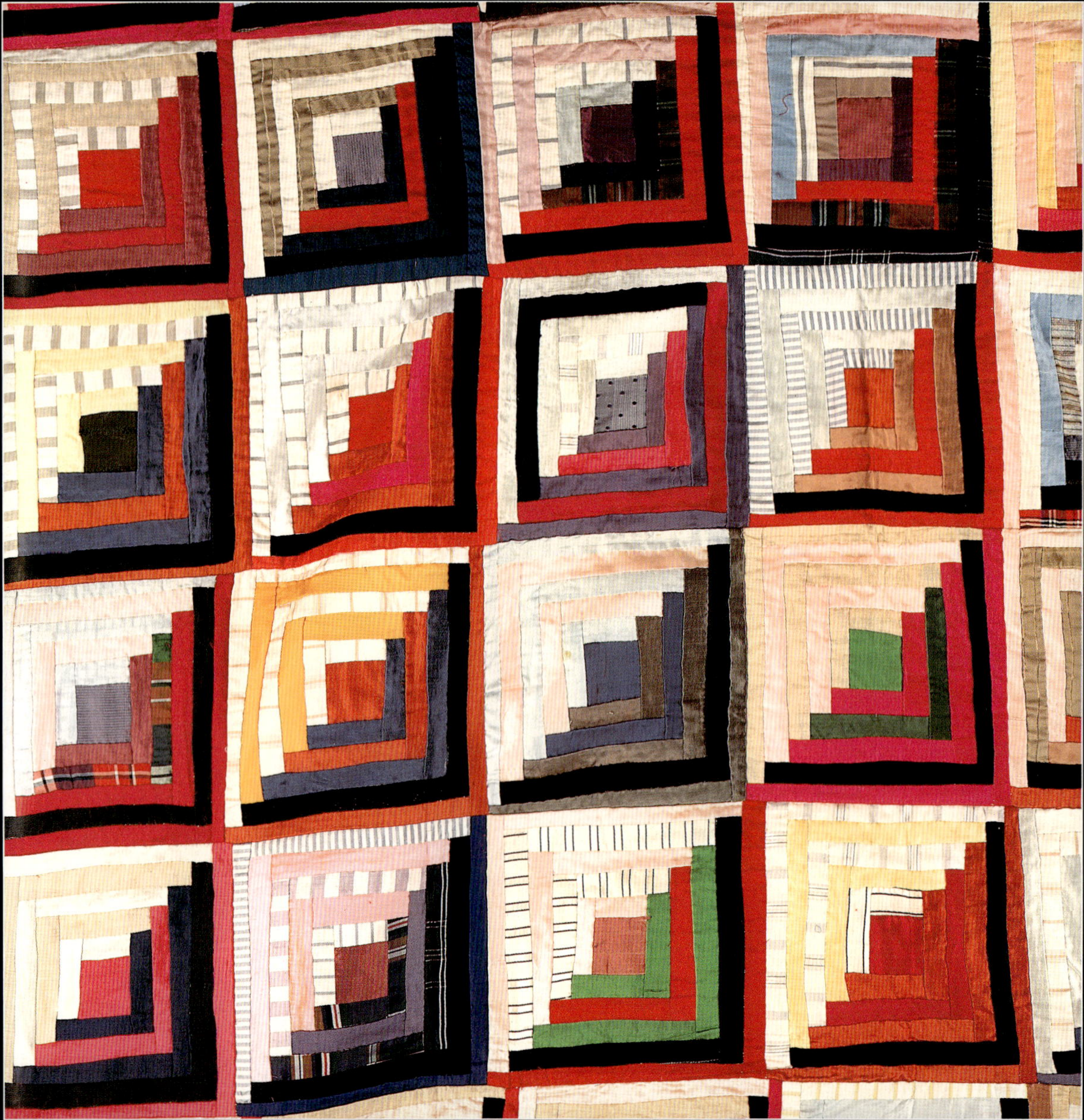

297

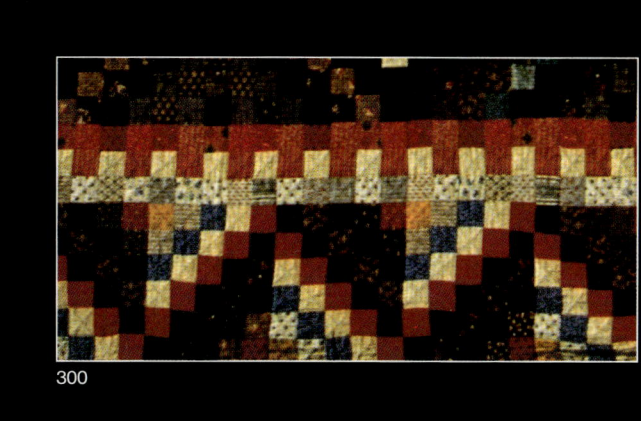

298

299

300

301

302

303

304

305

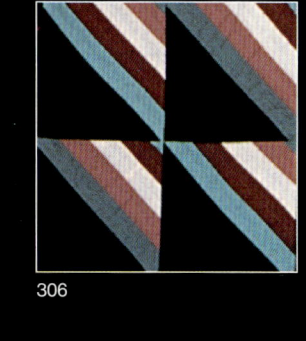

306

307

308

309

310

311

312

313

314

315

316

317 318 319 320
321 322 323 324
325 326 327 328

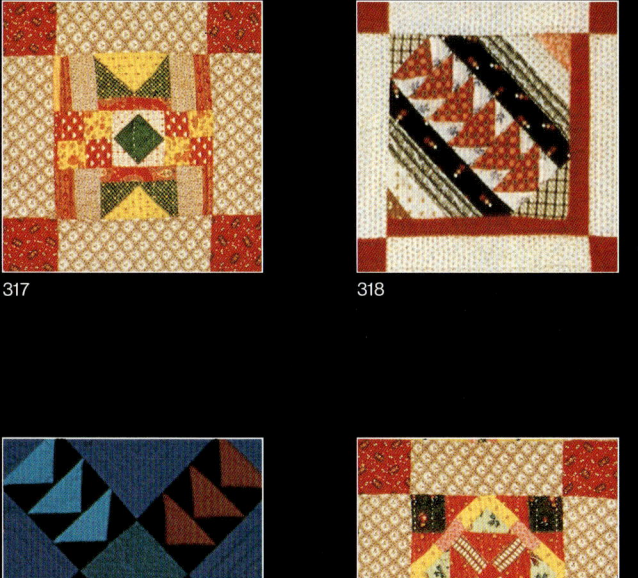

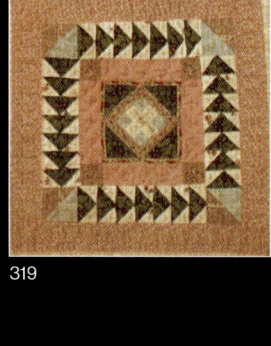

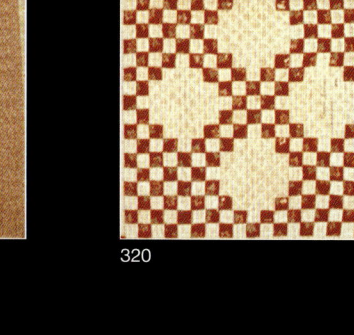

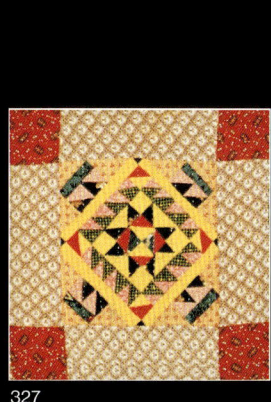

329

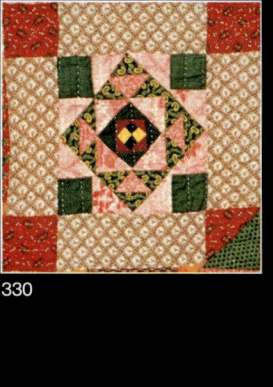

330

331

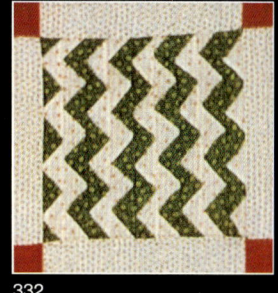

332

333

334

335

336

337

338

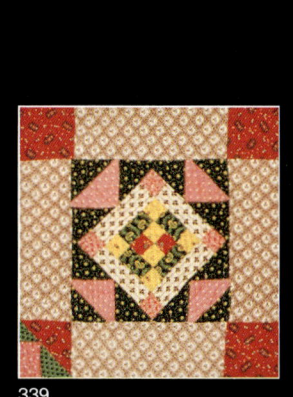

339

340

341

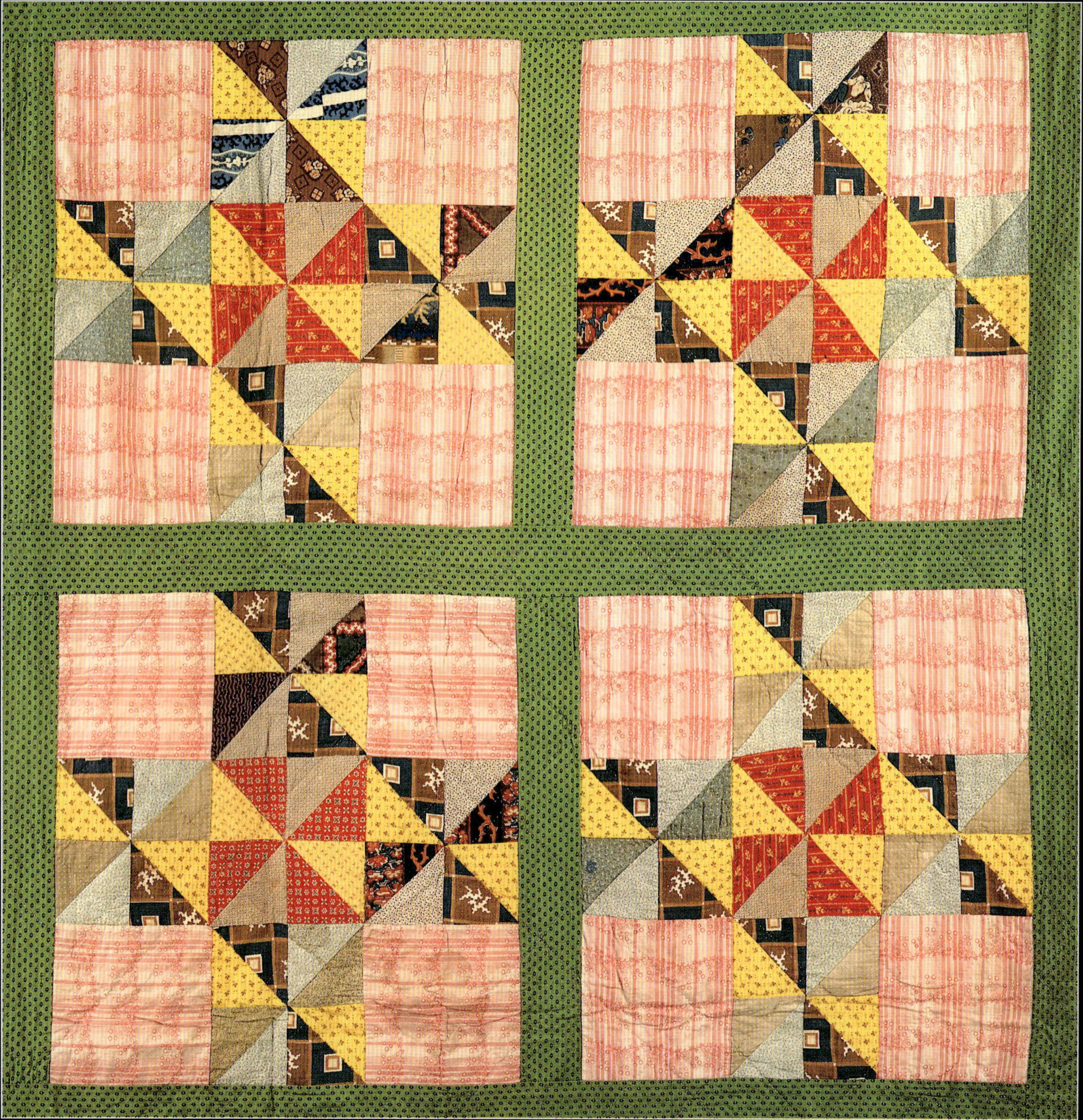

343

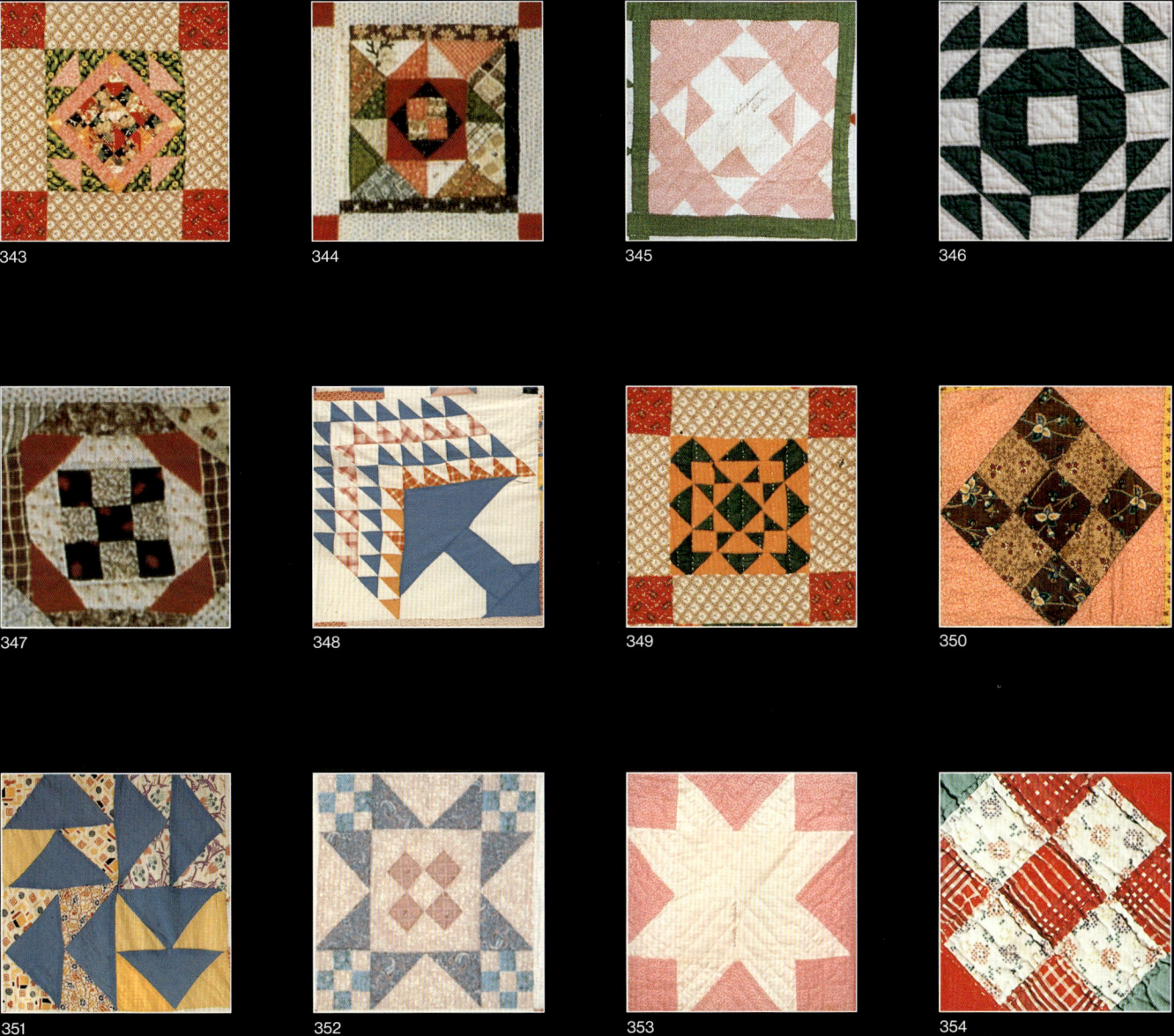

344

345

346

347

348

349

350

351

352

353

354

355

356

357

358

359

360

361

362

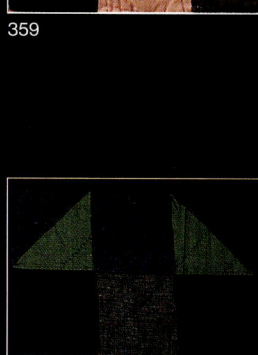

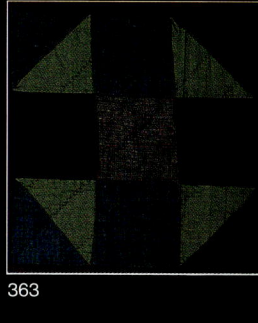

363

364

365

366

367

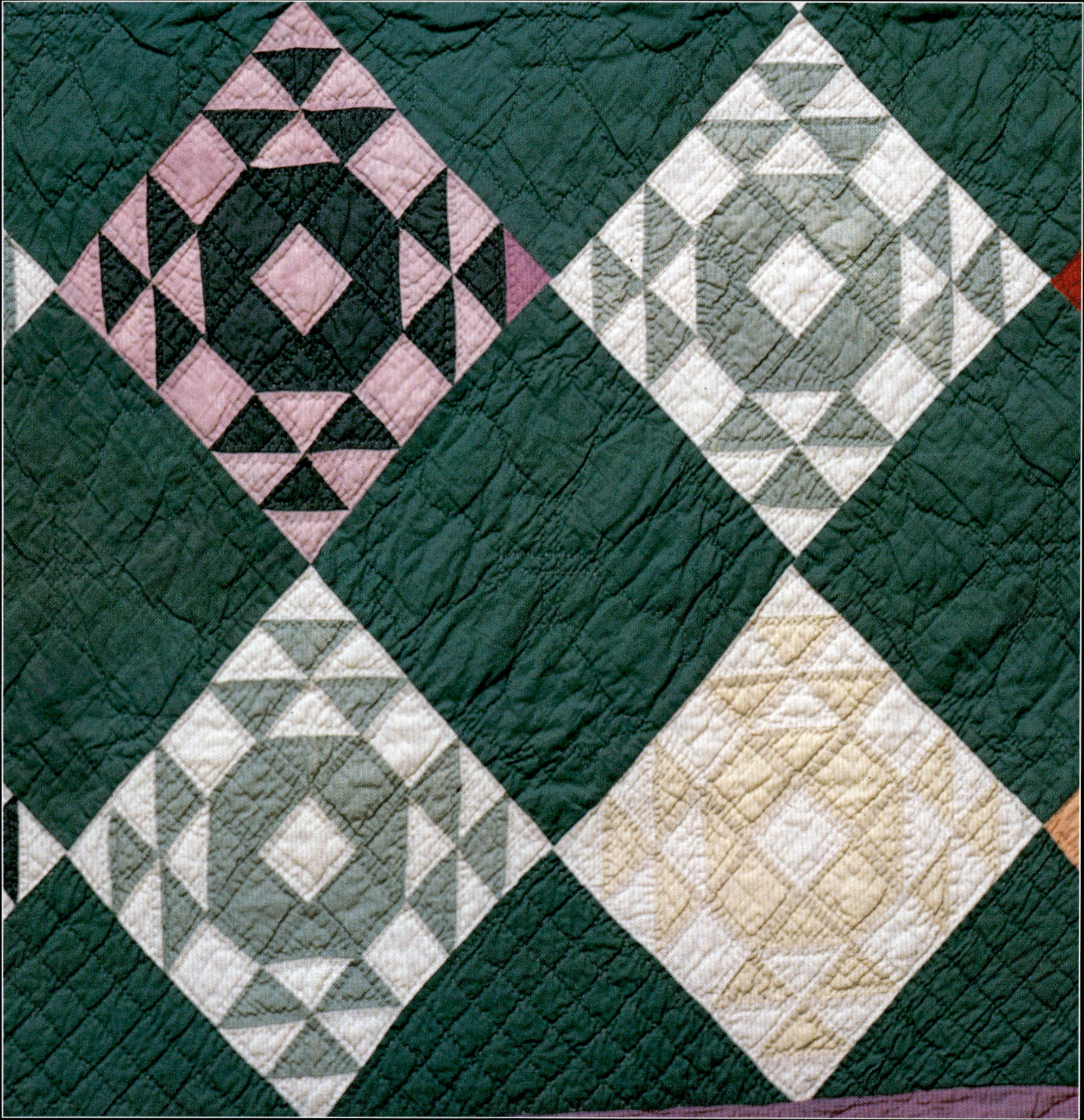

369
370
371
372
373
374
375
376
377
378
379
380

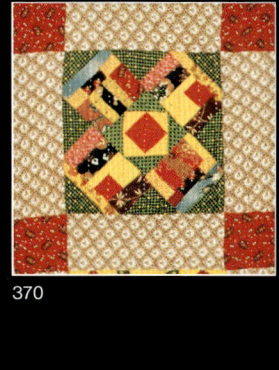

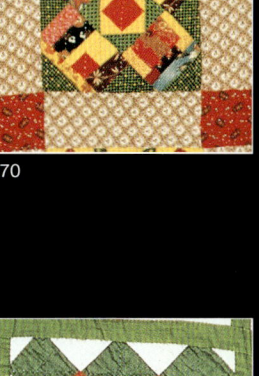

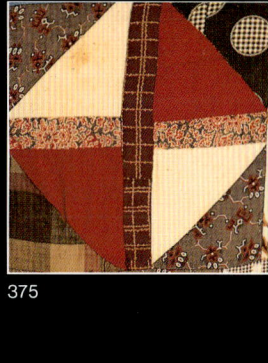

381

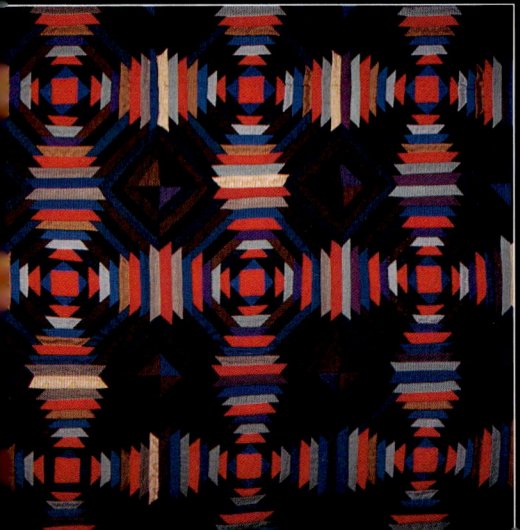

382

383

384

385 386 387 388

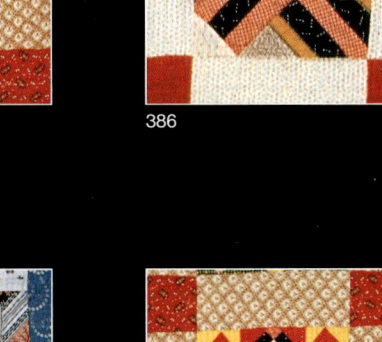

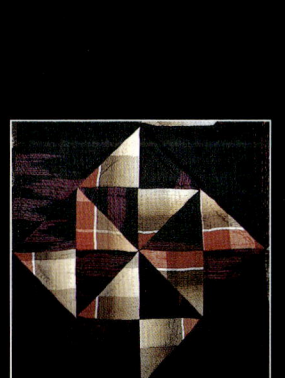

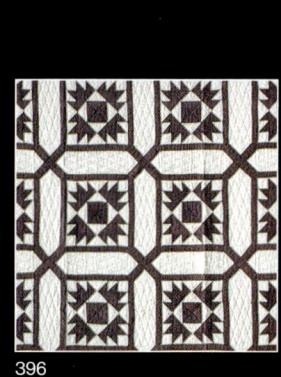

389 390 391 392

393 394 395 396

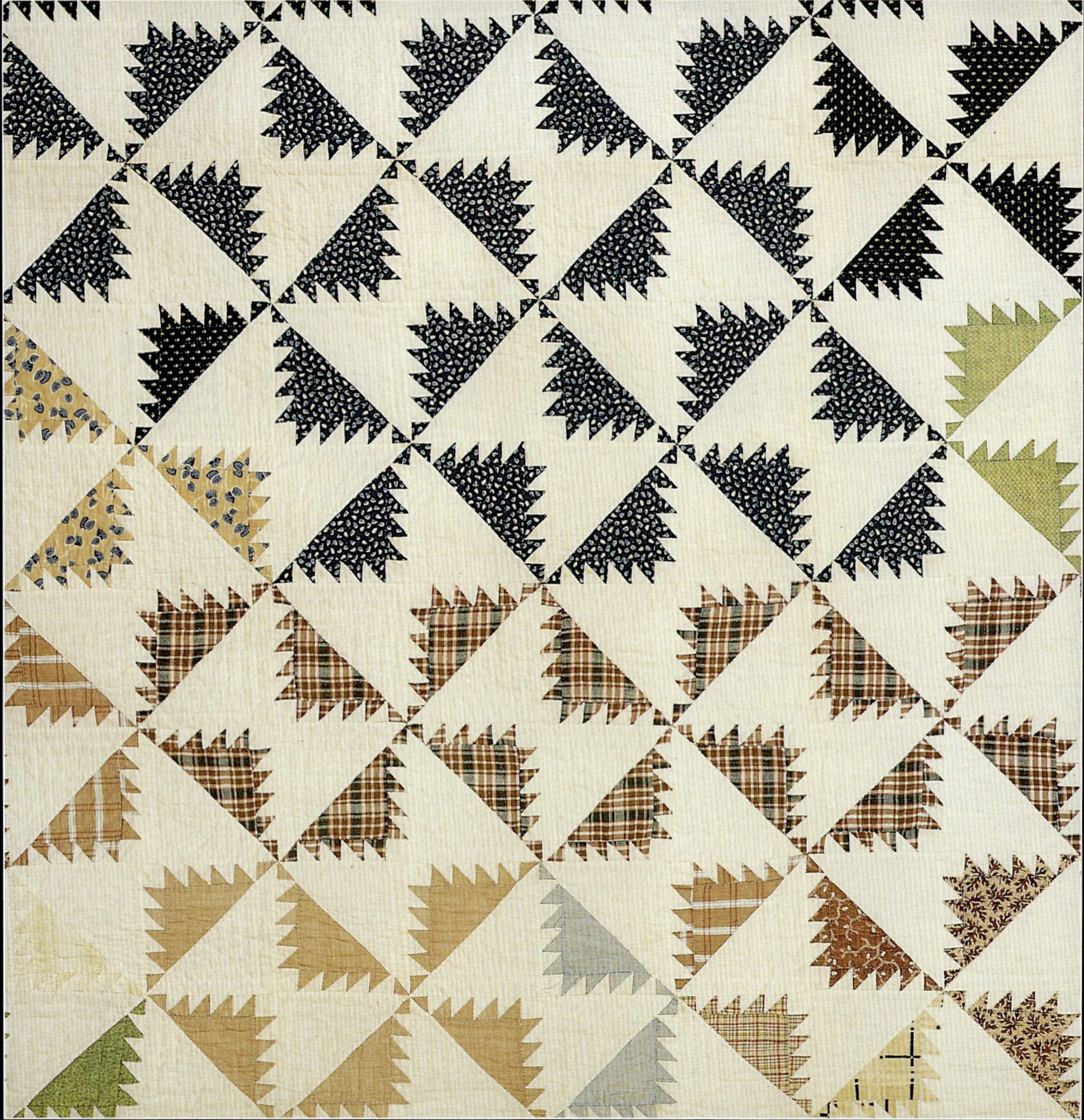

398

399

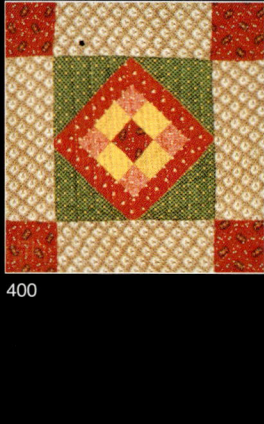

400

401

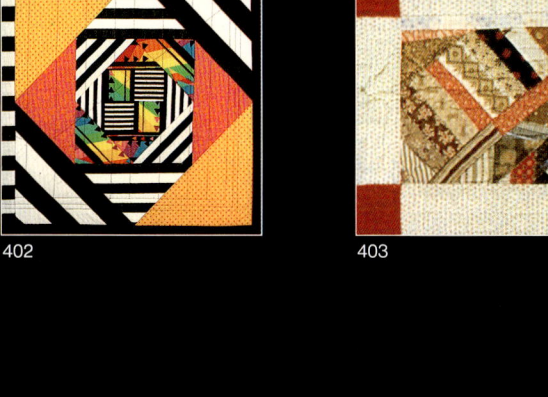

402

403

404

405

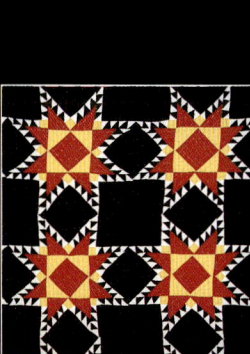

406

407

408

409

410 411 412 413

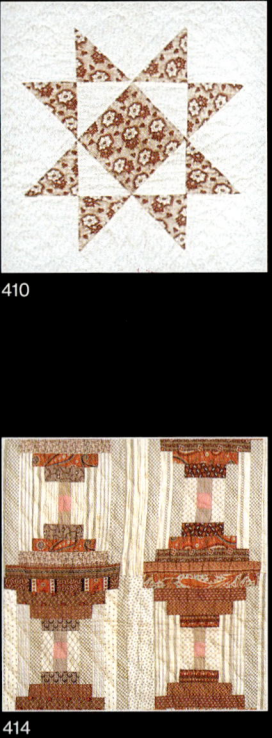

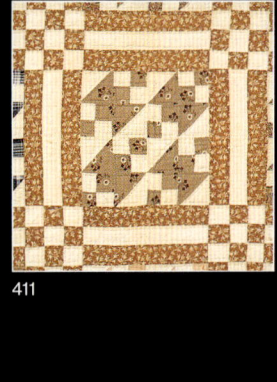

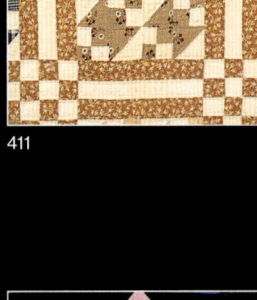

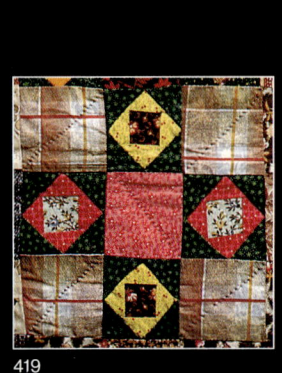

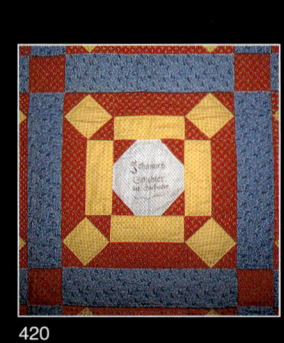

414 415 416 417

418 419 420 421

422

423

424

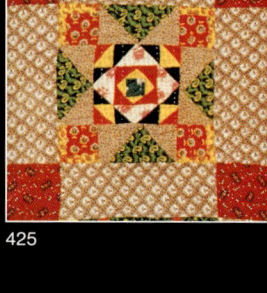

425

426

427

428

429

430

431

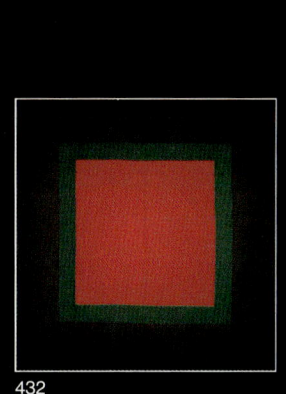

432

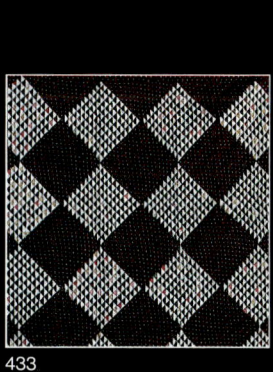

433

434

435

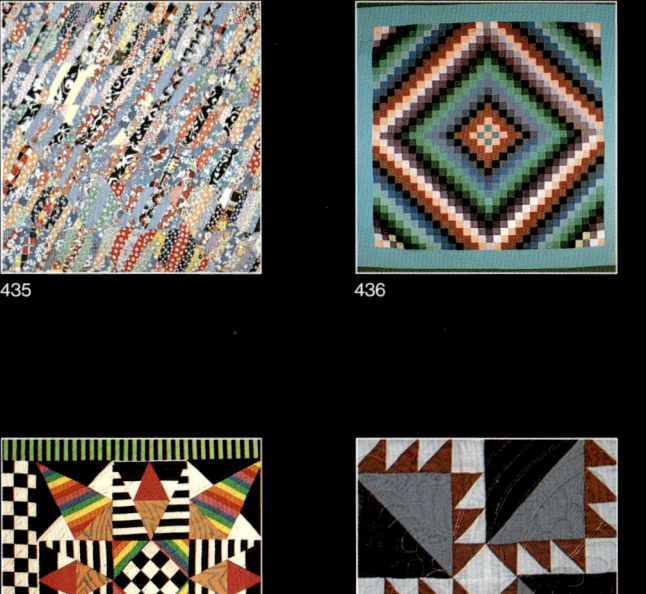

436

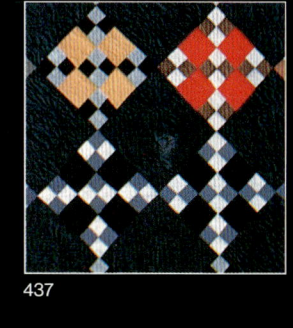

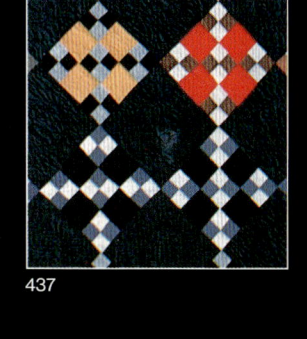

437

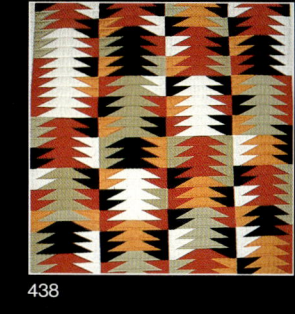

438

439

440

441

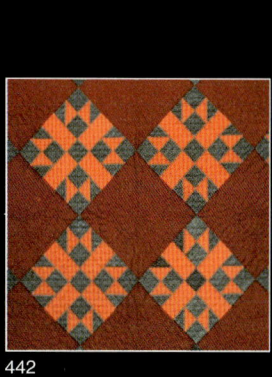

442

443

444

445

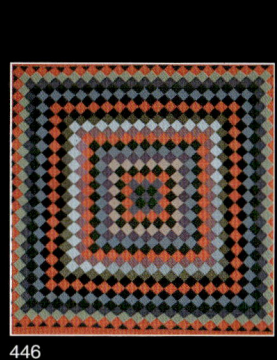

446

447

448

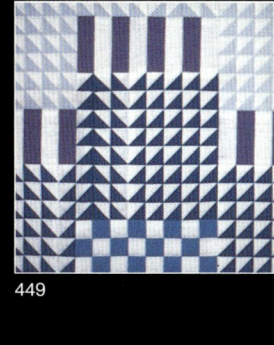

449

450

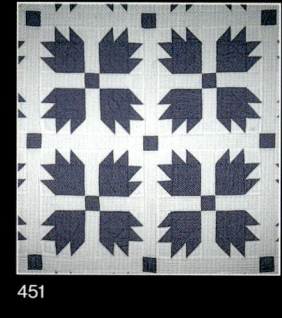

451

452

453

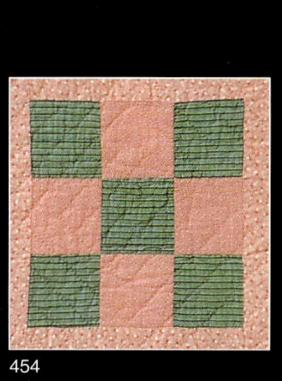

454

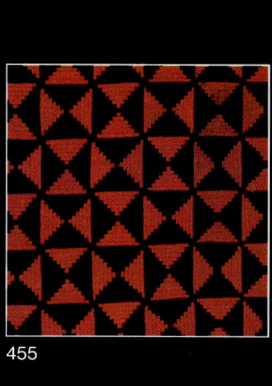

455

456

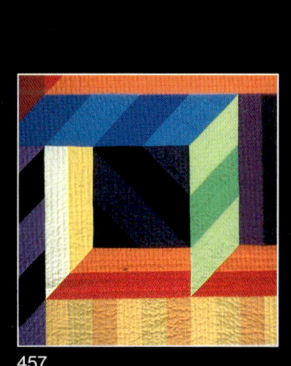

457

458

459

460

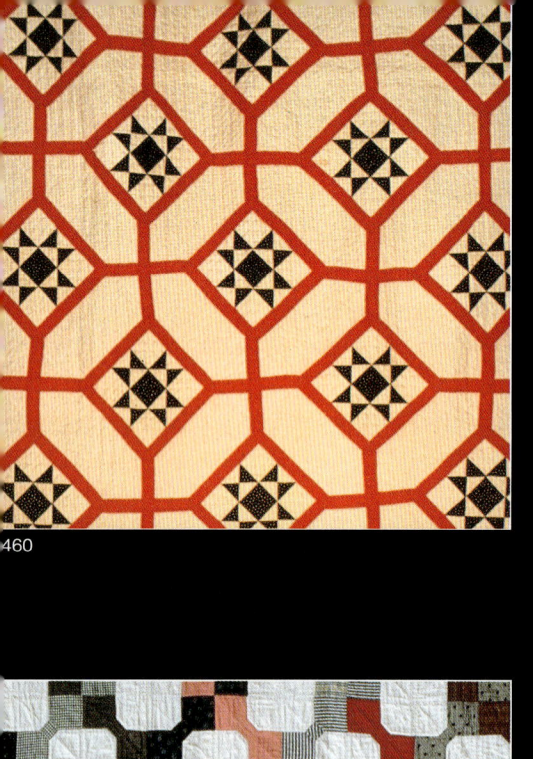

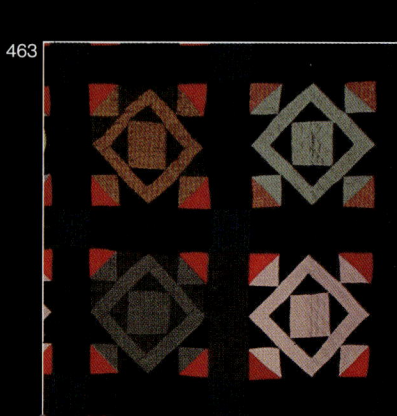

461

462

463

464

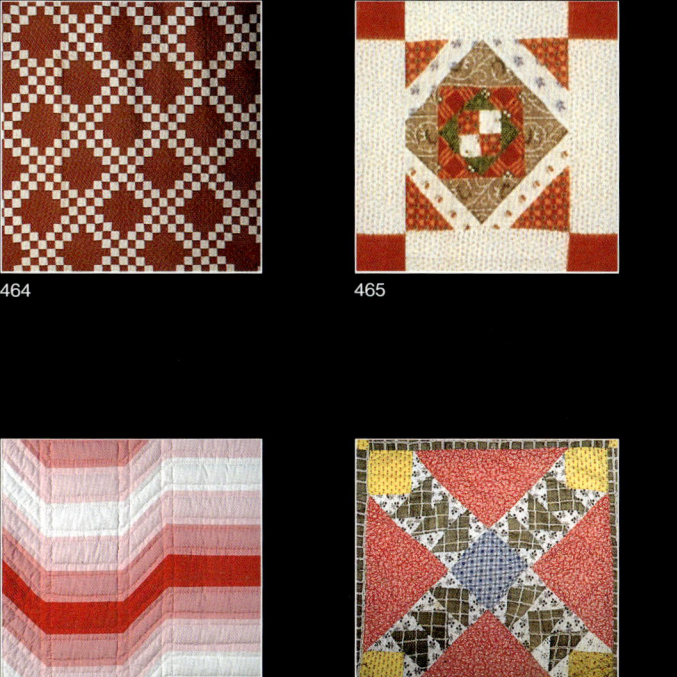

465

466

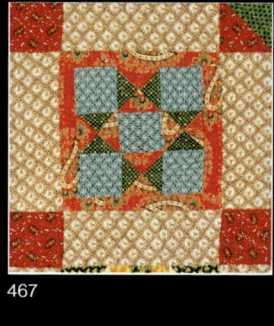

467

468

469

470

471

472

473

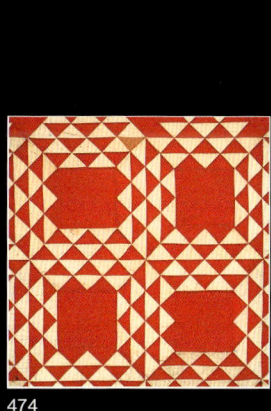

474

475

476

477 478 479 480

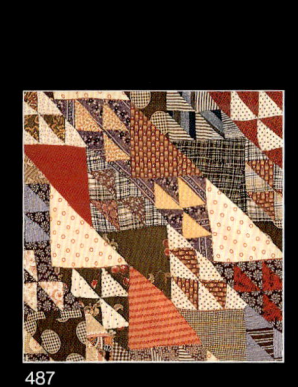

481 482 483 484

485 486 487 488

489

490

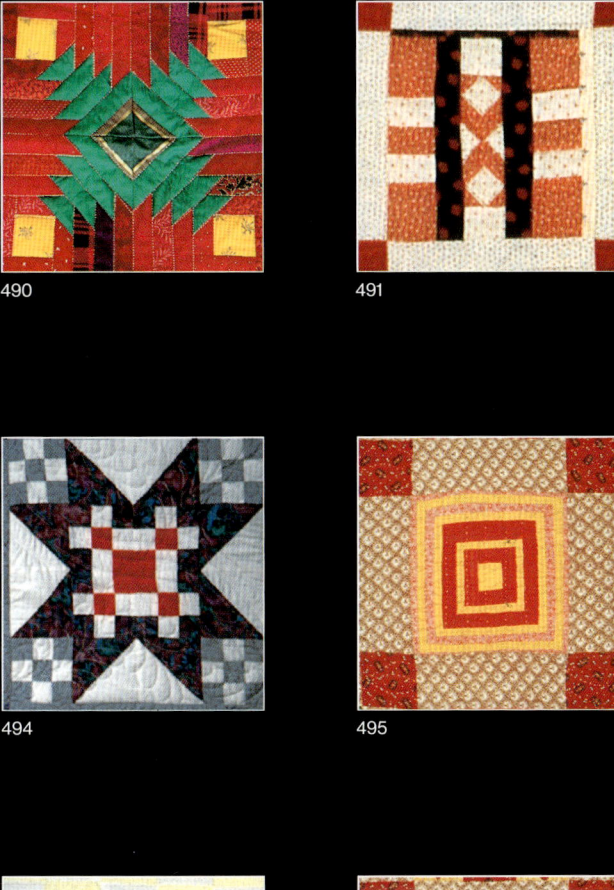

491

492

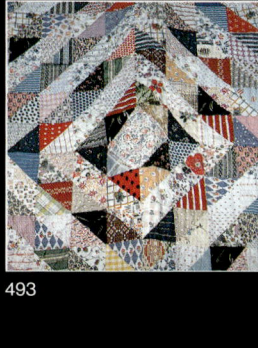

493

494

495

496

497

498

499

500

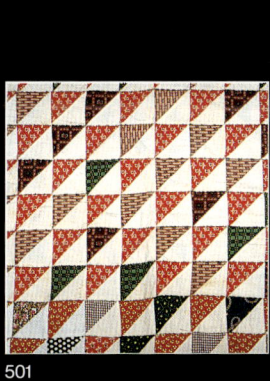

501

502

503

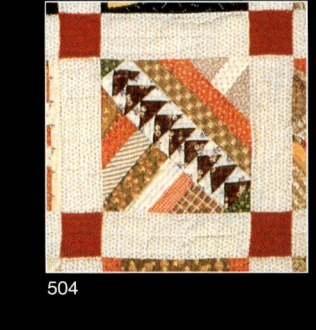

504

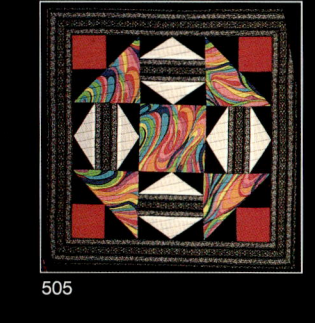

505

506

507

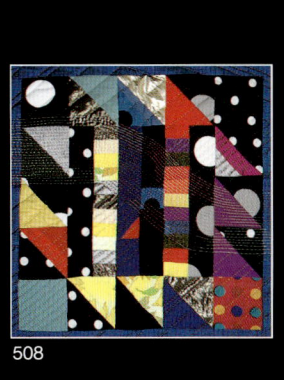

508

509

510

511

512

513

514

515

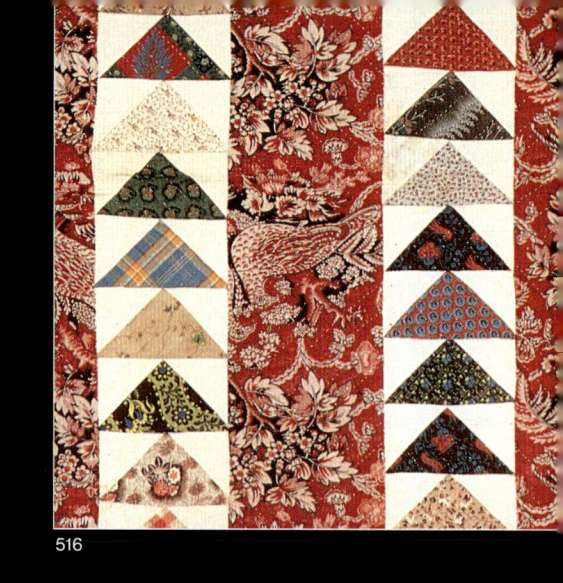

516

517

518

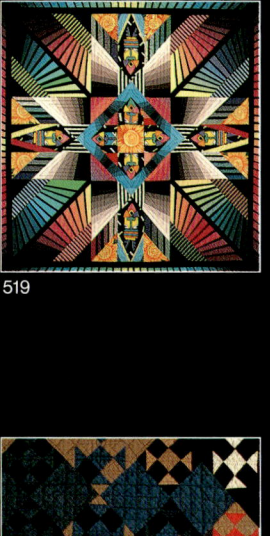

519

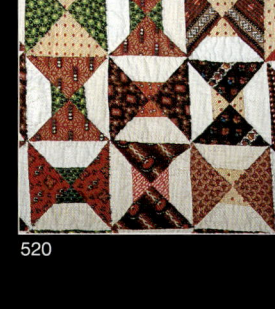

520

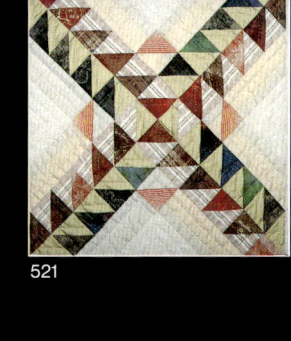

521

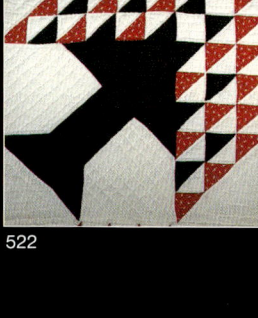

522

523

524

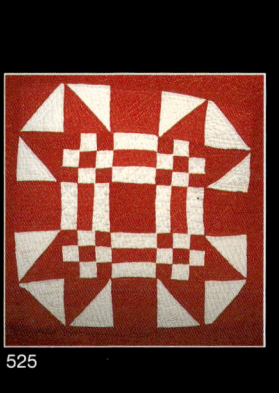

525

526

527

528

529

530

531

532

533

534

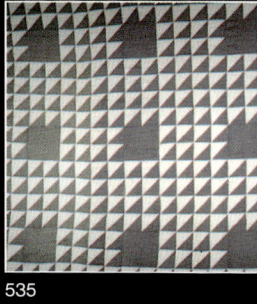

535

536

537

538

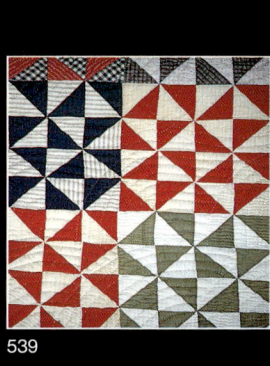

539

540

541

542

543

544 545 546 547

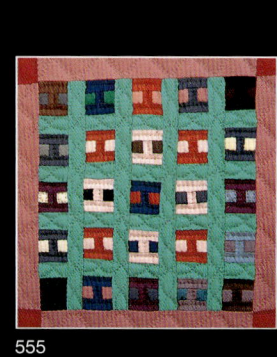

548 549 550 551

552 553 554 555

556

557

558

559

560

561

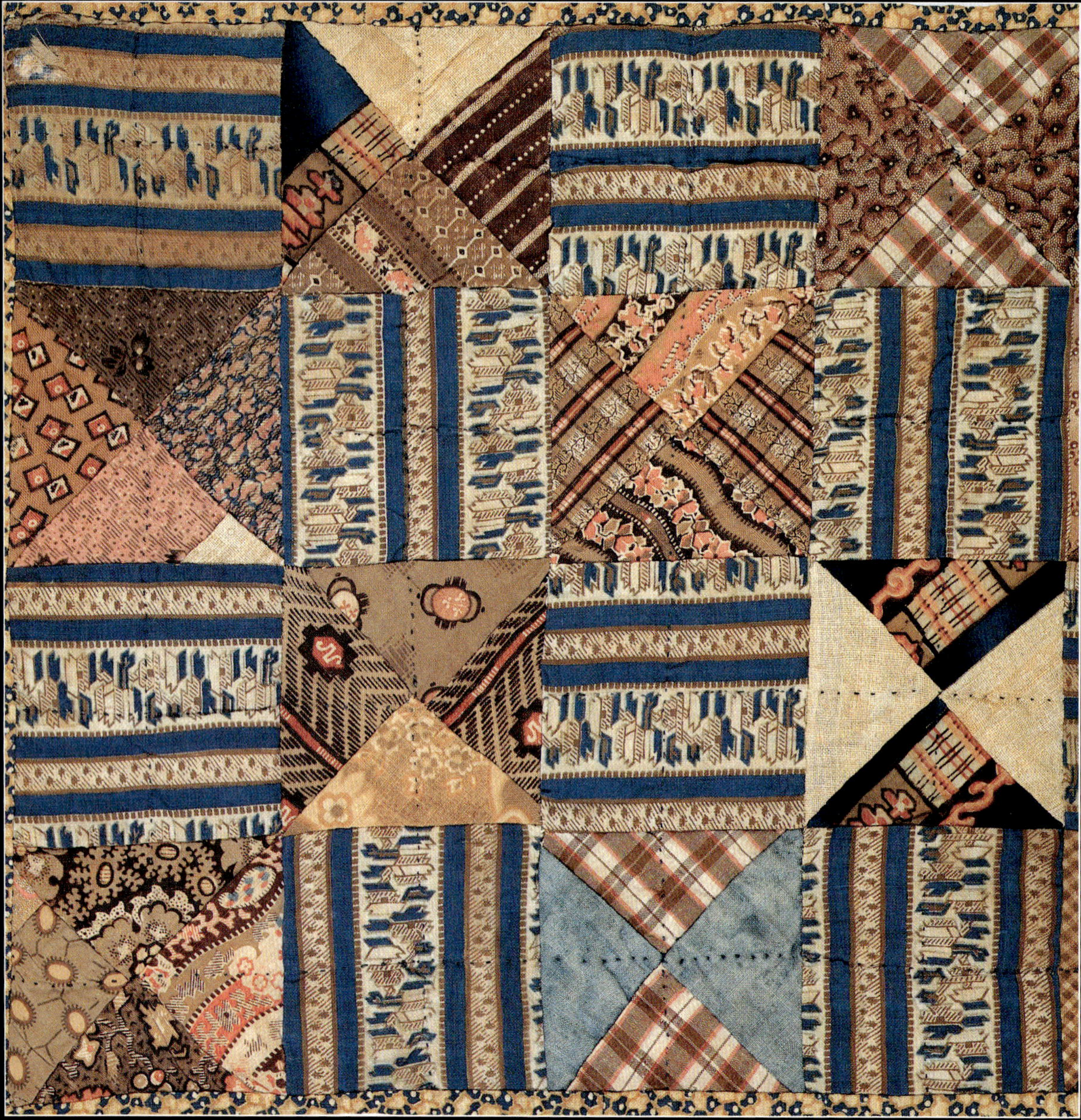

奥出直人 Naohito Okude, PH.D （おくで・なおひと） 慶応義塾大学環境情報学部助教授 Associate Professor Faculty of Environmental Information Keio University

19 30年代、フォークロアの掘り起こし、フォークトラディションの再構築が行われた。古都ウイリアムズバーグの考古学的な復元、保存。民具や歌の掘り起こしは失業対策の一環でもあった。

肉体労働をやめ都心のビルオフィスに勤め、徹底的にアメリカン・カントリー・スタイルの郊外の家に住むというのが、当時のアメリカ人の描いたヴィジョンである。

こうしてデザインされたアメリカ的テイストのホーム・デコレーションのなかで、キルトも象徴的な構成物のひとつとなり、消費アイテムとして流通した。

60年代、消費の中に転換された前の時代のフォークロアが、イン・フォークロアとして再び登場する。カウンター・カルチャーの世代に見直されたのである。

さまざまな伝統を集めた「アメリカ的」フォークロア、日「フェイクロア」は、すなわち大量生産されたものである。しかし、真のフォークロアには、別の知識が存在する、と。

ノスタルジーとして共同作業を捜し求めたり、近代を拒絶してフォークロアを検討しなおした。

例えば、アフロ・アメリカンの影響をクレージー・キルトに見る。ジャズと同じで、キルトという西洋の伝統にアフロ・アメリカンの伝統が融合し、オフ・ビートになった。

キルトの中にも文字に書かれなかったアメリ

In the 1930's there was a revival of folklore and folk traditions. The old city of Williamsburg was restored and preserved. This revival of folk crafts and songs were also a part of depression-era "make work" programs.

The ideal of the time was to escape manual labor. People wanted to work in a city office building and live in a suburban recreation of the American "country" home.

Quilts formed an important part of this American styleof home decoration and consequently become consumer goods.

In the 1960's the folk tradition of the previous - era, as changed through consumption, reemerged as "in" folklore and was reevaluated by the counterculture generation.

So-called "American forklore", which was seen as a hodgepodge of varying traditions, was called "fakelore" that is mass produced. However "genuine" folk was different.

Out of nostalgia this generation sought collective labor, rejected the modern age, and reevaluated folk traditions.

For example, the influence of Aflo-American can be seen in crazy quilts. As with jazz, a western tradition is merged with Aflo-American tradition to become something offbeat. American quilts can reveal much about

カの歴史が残っている。そこで、アカデミックな分野でも、キルト研究が始まり、スミソニアンもキルトのコレクションに意欲をみせた。

しかし、60年代的な意味での「本物のキルト」も、「本物の民芸」と同じようにマーケットを形成していった。

90年代の今、こうしたホームデコレーションカルチャーは、急速に場所を失いつつある。アメリカは、バナキュラーなものを捜し求めることをやめ、より洗練された尖ったものを強く指向しているように見える。

アメリカの良さは、「ちょっといい加減」なところにあると思うのだが。

American history. For this reason, academic study of quilts began, and such interests as the Smithsonian showed a new interest in acquiring quilt collections.

Eventually, a "real folk craft" market developed for the "genuine" quilts of the 1960's.

Now, in the 1990's, this home decoration culture is rapidly losing its place. America has stopped seeking the vernacular and has turned to the refined.

In my opinion the best of America is in its everyday quality.

THE PATCHWORK QUILT.

THE PATCHWORK QUILT.

THERE was a time when American housewives prided themselves on their neat and often elaborate patchwork quilts; and merry indeed were the "quilting-bees," when the women, young and old, married and single, used to gather at some neighbor's house to take a hand in the work. What a hum of voices, what cheery laughter, what plying of needles, made the afternoon pass swiftly, while the work progressed as if invisible hands assisted! How pleasant it was when evening came, and needles and thimbles and chalk and line and scissors were laid aside, and the cheerful hostess invited her friends into the clean, tidy kitchen to tea! Our thrifty ancestors were not ashamed to eat in the kitchen, where mothers, wives, and daughters did their own work, unplagued by servants. What abundance crowned the board!—the steaming tea-pot, hot "riz" biscuit, smoking from the oven, cream toast, three or four varieties of home-made cake, and preserves of every description—"sweetmeats," as they were generally termed. Besides the men-folks of the household, the minister was usually the only representative of the masculine sex; the husbands, brothers, and lovers came later in the evening, when all kinds of merry, harmless games were in order.

There are few parts of the country where this custom still lingers, cheap manufactures having superseded the necessity of this branch of domestic industry. Here and there may be found some old grandmother who still clings to the habits of her youthful days, and employs much of her time at the quilting-frame. The artist from whose skillful pencil the touching illustration on this page is engraved was fortunate enough in one of his New England rambles to discover a farm-house where the art has not yet become entirely a matter of tradition. The old lady, whose pleasant face he has faithfully transferred to his drawing, kindly gave him permission to sketch her while at work. She is a type of a race which is rapidly passing away under new conditions of society. The next generation will know them only by tradition, and by such pictures as the one we give on this page.

POVERTY.

PEOPLE who never were poor in the sense of absolute nothingness, being without money, and all prospect of having the necessities and decencies of their nature supplied, can not enter into the feelings that imbitter life. To be poor in this age is to be an outcast. Good and kind-hearted people pray, they imagine, very sincerely for those dependent beings, poor men, poor women, and poor children; but they have no objections to their transplantation in heaven. How few remember the poor after the fitful scenes of life are over with them! Neither their virtues, their miseries, nor their portraits are preserved. Poverty is no passport to good society. Who

1872年12月21日　ハーパーズ・ウィークリー紙 「パッチワーク　キルト」の記事から

December 21, 1872. HAPRER'S WEEKLY 「THE PATCHWORK QUILT」

87ページの説明

アメリカの主婦が自作の美しいキルトを自慢の種にした時代があった。老いも若きも、既婚未婚を問わず、近所の家に集まり一緒に針をもった。

話し声、ささやき笑い、せっせと動く針、午後の時間はあっという間に過ぎ、キルトが出来上がって行く。夕方には、針、指ぬき、チャコ、糸、はさみが並べ置かれ、その家の主婦が清潔に片付いた台所に招き入れてお茶をもてなす。

当時の女性たちは倹約家なので、台所でめいめい自由に食べるのに遠慮はない。食卓の上には、暖かいお茶、オーブンからは焼き上がったビスケットの煙、クリーム・トースト、三、四種類の自家製ケーキ、さまざまな砂糖漬け菓子などなど、いっぱいに並べられている。

家事の場面で、男性が受持つのは男らしい振舞いを示すことだけであることが多い：夫、兄弟、恋人たちは、陽気で無邪気なゲームが始まる夕方遅く集まって来る。

こうした風習が残っている地域が少ないのは、安価な工業製品にこの種の家内工業の必要性が駆逐されたからである。若い頃の習慣を守り、キルト枠に向かって過ごす時間が長いおばあさんをたまに見かけるぐらいである。幸いにもこの絵の画家は、この芸術が完全に伝統の中に埋没してはいないある農家を、ニュー・イングランドの散策で発見した。絵の中に満足げな顔を忠実に描かれたこの老婦人は、仕事中のスケッチを画家に許したのである。彼女は、急速な変化の中で消え行く種類の人間である。次の世代の人間は、ここに紹介した絵などによって伝統の中のこととしか知り得ないのであろう。（抄訳）

今からおよそ120年前の文章である。キルト作りや、キルティング・ビーが、廃れ行く慣習として説明されている。

しかし、一世紀以上を経た現在、キルト作りやキルティング・ビーは歴史の教科書でだけ知ることのできる「伝統」にはならなかった。

この時代から現在まで、さらなる幾たびかの熱狂の時代を繰り返し、おそらくこれ以後完成したキルトの数は、この記事の時代までの制作数をはるかに凌駕している。

もちろん、実用品を賄うための共同作業や、不足を補うための家内労働というキルトの制作動機は急速に衰えた。

例えば、農家の女性の現金収入の方途として、豊かさを誇る装飾品として、個性を競う作品として、多くの女性を魅了し作り続けられているのである。キルティング・ビーは、相互扶助と社交という二つの側面の、後者の比重が大きくなりはしたが、お茶とお菓子のもてなしの慣習と共に今に続いている。

また、このキルト作りやキルティング・ビーは、ヨーロッパにも逆輸出され、日本を始めとするアジア各国の女性達の間にも一部ながら定着している。

キルト作りがすぐに消え去る風習のように述べた記事がその後の歴史を予測し得なかったのとは逆に、この画家のスケッチは、現在も変わらぬキルターの姿を描き出している。思索に耽ける哲学者か宗教家のようにさえ似た充足した時間を過ごす満足の表情が、現在のキルターをも捉えてやまないキルト作りの魅力を説明してくれるのではないだろうか。

INDEX　　　　　　　　　　　　　　　　　　　　　　　　　　　　　索　引

ALBUM　アルバム
92　284　286　313　374　407　480　518

ALBUM STAR　アルバム・スター
16　255

ANVIL　かな床
186

THE ARKANSAS STAR　アーカンサスの星
667

AUSTIN　オースチン
210

BAR　バー
110　333

BARRISTER'S BLOCK　弁護士のブロック
291

BASKET　バスケット
415　471　529

BEAR'S PAW　熊の手
41　451

BIG DIPPER　北斗七星
119

BOW TIE　ボー・タイ
175　462

BRICKS　れんが
289

BROKEN DISHES　こわれた皿
46　69　71　113　323　387　455

CARD TRICK　カード・トリック
33

CENTER DIAMOND　センター・ダイヤモンド
8

CENTER SQUARE　センター・スクエア
432

CHECKERBORD　チェッカーボード（市松）
485

CHEVRON　シェブロン（山形）
389

CHIMNEY SWEEP　煙突掃除
242　502

CHRISTIAN CROSS　クリスチャン・クロス
13　29　57　62　111　261

CORN AND BEANS　コーンと豆
174　281

COTTON REEL　糸巻
484

CRIMSON RAMBLER　深紅のばら
85

CRISSCROSS　十字
437

CROSS　十字架
50　413

CRAZY ANN　クレージー・アン
72

DAVIL'S CLAW　悪魔の爪
223

DIAGONAL CHECKERBOARD　斜めチェッカーボード
489

DIAGONAL TRIANGLES　斜め三角
501　556

DOUBLE IRISH CHAIN　ダブル・アイリッシュ・チェーン
464　514　527　557　560

DOUBLE NINE—PATCH　ダブル・ナインパッチ
279

DOUBLE PINWHEEL　二重風車
184

DOUBLE SAWTOOTH　二重のこぎり歯
361

DOUBLE X　ダブル X
171　180　381　530

DOUBLE Z　ダブル Z
394

DRESDEN PLATE　ドレスデンの皿
238

DRUNKARD'S PATH　よっぱらいの道
173

ECONOMY NINE—PATCH　倹約ナイン—パッチ
419

FANNY'S FAN　ファニーの扇
154

FEATHERED STAR　フェザー・スター
226　282　336　406　476　544

54—40 OR FIGHT　54度40分さもなくば戦いを
55　293

FIVE STRIPES　ファイブ・ストライプ
153

FLOCK　鳥の群
506

FLYING BATS　飛ぶこうもり
511

FLYING X　飛ぶ X
395

FOUR PATCH　フォー・パッチ
30　49　66　67　190

GENTLEMAN'S FANCY　紳士のお気に入り
371

GEORGETOWN CIRCLE　ジョージタウン・サークル
285　295　346　360　368

GOOSE IN THE POND　池のがちょう
552

GRANDMOTHER'S CROSS　おばあさんの十字架
99

HANDS ALL AROUND　ハンズ・オール・アラウンド
114

HOVERING HAWKS　空を飛ぶ鷹
358

HANDY ANDY　器用なアンディ
142

INCLINED ROG CABIN　傾いたログ・キャビン
22

INDIAN TRAILS　インディアンの足跡
367　397

IRISH PUZZLE　アイリッシュ・パズル
124

JACK IN THE BOX　びっくり箱
56

JACOB'S LADDER　ヤコブのはしご
215　411　500　528

KANSAS TROUBLE　カンサス・トラブル
440

LETTER H　H
555

LITTLE SAW TOOTH　小さなのこぎりの歯
14

MOSAIC　モザイク
278　362　453

MRS. TAFT'S CHOICE　タフト婦人の好み
475

NINE—PATCH　ナインパッチ
　7　98　107　120　149　151　165　178
188　213　227　237　252　256　276　294
303　305　307　326　331　347　340　350
351　354　359　376　400　412　454　467
472　487　509　513　536　538　553　554

NORTHERN LIGHTS　北極光
164

OCEAN WAVE　オーシャン・ウェーブ
474　526

ODD FELLOW'S PATCH　オッド・フェローズ・パッチ
283

OHIO STAR　オハイオ・スター
6　68　189　272　328

OLD CROW　老がらす　408

91

PHILADELPHIA PAVEMENT　フィラデルフィアの舗道

15

PINEAPPLE　パイナップル

197　198　216　383

PINE TREE　松ノ木

496

PINWHEEL　かざぐるま

128　275　308　342　416　510　539

POSTAGE STAMP　切手

98　246　314　378

PUSS IN THE CORNER　隅っこの小猫

43　302　134　233　302　458

RAIL FENCE　柵

33　269

RAINBOW　虹

83　177

RETURN OF THE SWALLOWS　帰ってきた燕

351

RISING STAR　昇る日

418

ROG CABIN　ログ・キャビン

　　1　　4　　5　19　20　25　26　31
　34　48　63　64　67　81　108　116
135　199　273　296　414　355　534

ROMAN STRIPE　ローマン・ストライプ

36　306

ROAD TO PARIS　パリへの道

181

SAVE ALL　全員救出

461

SAW TOOTH　のこぎりの歯

38　143　277

SHOOFLY　ハエしっし

363　434

SINGLE IRISH CHAIN　シングル・アイリッシュ・チェーン

9

SISTER'S CHOICE　姉さんの好み

222

SKY ROCKET　スカイ・ロケット

115　254

SNOWFLAKE　雪片

195

SPIDER WEB　くもの巣

80

SPOOLS　糸巻

137　520

SQUARE DEAL　公正取引

430

SQUARES 四角
122

SQUARES IN SQUARES 四角の中の四角
17

ST. ANDREW'S CROSS 聖アンドリューの十字架
274 382

STAR FLOWER スター・フラワー
18   44   158   169   207   268   353   377
507   533

STEPPING STONES ころがる石
549

STREAK OF LIGHTNING 稲妻
247   332

SUNSHINE AND SHADOW 日向と日陰
11   12   21   148   209   316   422   436   446

SWASTIKA かぎ十字
53   479

TEXAS STAR テキサス・スター
562

THOUSAND PYRAMID たくさんの三角
426   459

TREE 木
348   522

TREE EVERLASTING 永久の木 428

TRIP AROUND THE WORLD 世界一周
24

TURNSTILE 回転木戸
259

UNION SQUARE ユニオン・スクエア
396

VARIABLE STAR 変光星
181   545

WEATHERVANE 風見
106   125

WHITE HOUSE STEPS ホワイトハウスの階段
495

WILD GOOSE CHASE 雁追い
10   159   266   271   287   321   417   447
516   543

ZIGZAG ジグザグ
421

93

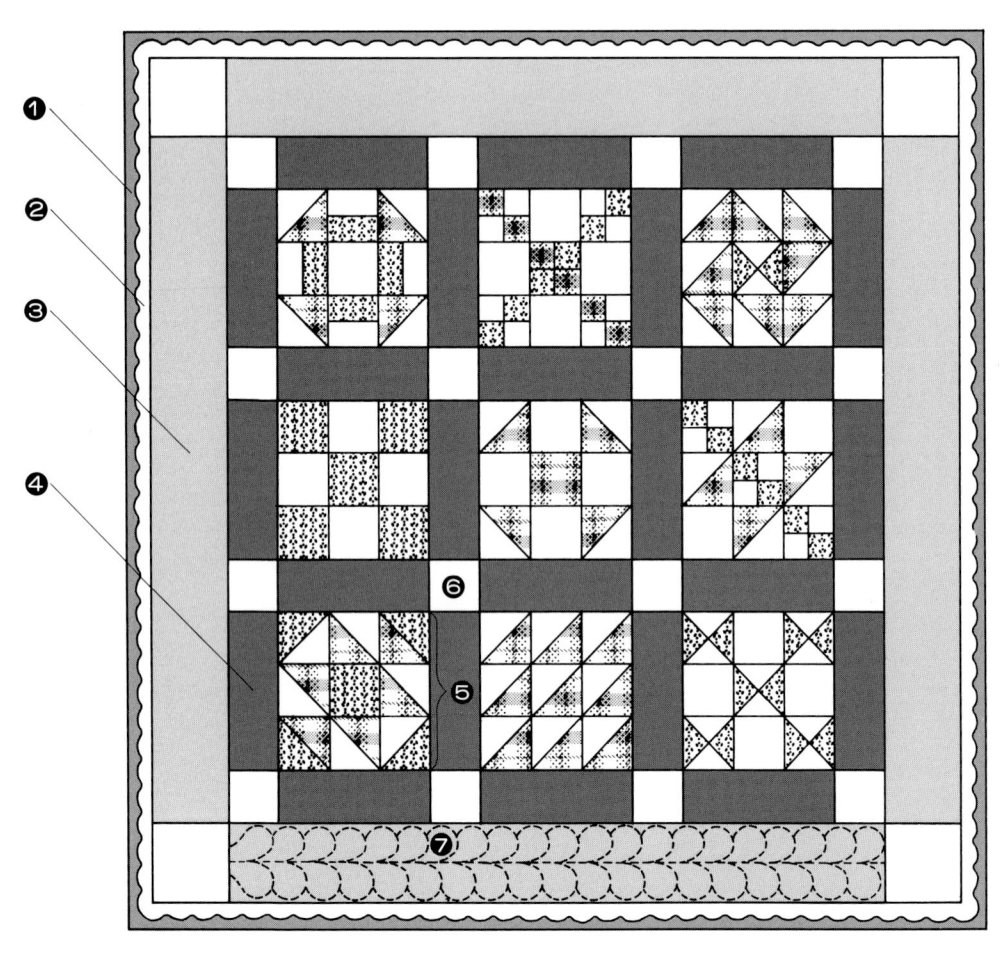

① 裏布 Backing　② キルト綿 Batting　③ ボーダー Border　④ サッシュ Sashing
⑤ ブロック Block　⑥ ポスト Post　⑦ キルティング デザイン Quilting Desing

参考文献
Selected Bibliography

Yvonne M. Khin. The collector's Dictionary ob QUILT NAMES & PATTERNS.
ACROPOLIS BOOKS LTD. Washington D.C. 1980

Judy Rehmel. THE QUILT I.D. BOOK. Prentice Hall Press. N.Y. 1986

本書に協力頂いた次の方々に御礼を申し上げます。
Very special thanks go to the following people :

アメリカン・フラー	AMERICA HURRAH
アーディス&ロバート・ジェームス夫妻	ARDIS & ROBERT JAMES
ベティ・ウルフ	BETTY WOLFE
キャリル・ブライヤー・ファラート	CARYL BRYER FALLERT
グゼニア・コード	XENIA CORD
ジーン・レイ・ローリー	JEAN RAY LAURY
ローラ・フィッシャー	LAURA FISHER
マサヨ・ヘンダーソン	MASAYO HENDERSON
ロデリコ E. キラコフ	RODERICK E. KIRACOFE
シェリー・ジガート	SHELLY ZEGART
イボンヌ・ポーセラ	YVVONE PORCELLA
鳥屋厳美	ITSUMI TORIYA
郷家啓子	KEIKO GOUKE
中原啓子	KEIKO NAKAHARA
後藤紀代子	KIYOKO GOTO
馬場雅子	MASAKO BABA
永井正子	MASAKO NAGAI
田宮雅子	MASAKO SHIMANO
窪田美土里	MIDORI KUBOTA
三沢幹子	MIKIKO MISAWA
服部利恵子	RIEKO HATTORI
長谷川幸子	SACHIKO HASEGAWA
島野徳子	TOKUKO SHIMANO
渡辺とみの	TOMINO WATANABE
熊部斗南	TONAMI KUMABE
佐藤ウメ	UME SATOU
英　訳：トーマス・フェルナー	TOMASU FHELNER
撮影協力：遠藤長光	NAGAMITSU ENDO
レイアウト：鈴木　真	MAKOTO SUZUKI

キルト・ブロックス①	
発行	1994年4月10日
監修・編集	吉武泰子
発行者	藤岡　護
発行所	株式会社 京都書院
	〒604 京都市中京区堀川通三条上ル
	TEL. 075-344-0053　FAX. 075-344-0099
企画	水野忠始
制作	漂蒼庵（京都書院）
印刷製本	日本写真印刷株式会社

QUILT BLOKS Vol.1	
Date of Publicalion	April 10, 1994
Editor	Yasuko Yoshitake
Publisher	Kyoto Shoin Co., Ltd.
	Sanjyo-agaru, Horikawa, Nakagyo-ku, Kyoto, Japan.
	Tel. 075-344-0053　Fax. 075-344-0099
Planner	Tadashi Mizuno
Printed and bound	Nissha Printing Co., Ltd.

Copyright © 1994 Yasuko Yoshitake Printed in Japan
ISBN4-7636-3219-1
All rights reserved, No part of this publication may be reproduced or transmitted in any form or by any means, electric or mechanical, including photographying recording or any information storage and retieval system now known or to be invented without permission in writing from the publisher.